THE NEXT STEP

ADJUSTING FROM STUDENT TO CHIROPRACTOR

Chidi Lynn

THE NEXT STEP

The Next Step

First Edition

(paperback)

ISBN 978-0-9955963-0-6

Self-published in Great Britain by Chidi Lynn

through REDBAK Publishing.

Copyright© Chidi Lynn 2017

The right of Chidi Lynn to be identified as the author of this work has been asserted in accordance with the Copyright Designs and Patents Act 1988.

All rights reserved.

This book is sold subject to the condition that it shall not, by way of trade or otherwise, be lent, re-sold, hired out or otherwise circulated without the author's prior consent in any form of binding or cover other than that in which it is published and without a similar condition, including this condition, being imposed on the subsequent purchase.

REDBAK Publishing

United Kingdom

Printed in United Kingdom

Cover Design by

Julia Russell

Contents

List of exercises: v

About the Author vi

Acknowledgements ix

Introduction 1

STEP 1 – Job Searching 4

    Competition 5

    Jobs 5

    Clarity 6

STEP 2 – Applying for Jobs 12

    Covering Letter 12

        Letter Format 13

        Letter Content 16

    Curriculum Vitae (CV) 22

        Format and Content of CV 22

        CV Checklist: 25

        CV Example 27

STEP 3 – Interview Process 30

    Preparing for the interview 30

        Clothes 30

        Plan your Journey 31

    On Arrival 31

THE NEXT STEP

    Awaiting Interview 32

    Observation 33

    Post Interview Questions 38

    The Area 39

STEP 4 – Registrations 42

    Chiropractic Associations 43

    Chiropractic Insurance 46

    General Chiropractic Council (GCC) 48

    Royal College of Chiropractors (RCoC) 54

    European Chiropractors' Union (ECU) 54

    HMRC (If becoming self-employed) 55

    Bank 56

    Accountant 58

STEP 5 – Financial Management 64

    Post-graduation Expenditure 64

    Business Financial Management 70

    Personal Financial Management 71

    Student Loan 72

STEP 6 – Annual Responsibilities 76

    Continuing Professional Development (CPD) 76

    HMRC 79

        Book-keeping 79

THE NEXT STEP

    Tax Return 80

    National Insurance 82

    Income tax 83

    VAT 83

STEP 7 – Being True to You! 86

Index of Websites (in alphabetical order) 89

THE NEXT STEP

List of exercises:

Exercise 1: Your Chiropractic Vision 7
Exercise 2: Your Ideal Practice Overview 8
Exercise 3: Create a Covering Letter 15
Exercise 4: Create a CV 26
Exercise 5: Interview Questions 34
Exercise 6: Extra Interview Questions 37
Exercise 7: Your Ideal Area 39
Exercise 8: Association Exploration 45
Exercise 9: Insurance Cover 47
Exercise 10: GCC Requirements 51
Exercise 11: PRT Programme 54
Exercise 12: HMRC Registration 55
Exercise 13: Bank Registration 57
Exercise 14: Accountant Questions 61
Exercise 15: Financial Overview 69
Exercise 16: Expenditure Sheet Overview 69
Exercise 17: Student Loan Management 74
Exercise 18: CPD Preparation 77
Exercise 19: Book Keeping 80
Exercise 20: Tax Return 82

About the Author

During her time at the Anglo European College of Chiropractic, Chidi found it difficult balancing life as a student: preparing for the final exit exams, assignment deadlines, being Student Union President, applying for jobs, attending interviews alongside managing patients, and mentoring her clinic intern to fill her role once she graduated.

During this manic period she realised there were no guidelines for graduating and preparing for the bigger world as a chiropractor. Many students felt overwhelmed, confused and even fearful of what was to be done in the final months of college.

The greatest obstacle they faced was a poor understanding of the processes and procedures involved in registrations, job applications and starting their new life as a chiropractor. As Academic Representative for four years prior, Chidi gathered all reliable information and relayed it to the final year students. She took on the task of seeking answers to questions she and most students were asking: how, what, where from, to whom, by when and in what order?

Upon graduating, using that knowledge, she applied for eight jobs – receiving seven offers.

Through a lack of experience, she took jobs she thought were perfect, but ended realising they weren't for her because of mismatched abilities, interests, personality and values. She

THE NEXT STEP

believed it was her own failings, but became aware it was the entrepreneur in her wanting to do it her own way.

Now, years on, and owning her own successful practice, she's recorded her experiences, brought them up to date, and written them into a book, so that others who follow will find a suitable job without all the hassle she experienced!

THE NEXT STEP

All information within this book is up-to-date when going to print. Please check the relevant organisations and websites listed at the end of this book for further information if you are reading this at a later date.

Acknowledgements

I thank everybody who helped me on this journey. It has been one of self-discovery and enabled me to retrieve all I've learned and put it on paper.

Special thanks to Sandie, Arvid, Michaela, Abdul, Chantal and Miles who have encouraged, queried, read, edited and given constructive feedback to the content of this book. Without your support, this book would not have been made.

Thank you to my Dad, supporting me through my development, teaching me my first steps, and enabling me to get this far in life! Realistically, I wouldn't be where I am today without you, and as you said, 'everything you've done in your life is useful in some way or another,' which has proven true for this book.

Thank you, John. My rock! Without you, many things would not have happened! Your strength and belief in me, has inspired me to persevere and achieve all I set out to.

Thank you all for being part of my journey and most of all for believing in me when I struggled. Each challenge has certainly shaped me, and each door that closed allowed better ones to open.

I am, who I am, because of what was; I will be, who I can be, because of your support!

Love you all and thank you for being there.

Chidi x

Introduction

If like me, upon entering Chiropractic College, you probably had a vision of *how* you were going to work, *what* you were going to do and *why* you started this new venture. Along the way, with academics, various political views, personal stresses, deadlines and unexpected hurdles; the dream you first started with, may have become distorted to a smudged canvas of confusion. The goals, visions and dreams become supplanted by 'pass the exams and get out' instead of enabling your dream job – making a difference and a living.

This is a step-by-step guide to searching for the ideal job, working in a practice that suits your style of Chiropractic and growing as a practitioner. This book hopes to inspire you to become an impactful person and to bring out the Chiropractor within, who adds real worth and value to the profession. It will give you a deeper insight and help you become more focussed, productive and prepared for the journey ahead.

Each step works sequentially to build on previous steps. The journey begins prior to the interview stage, building momentum, to the day when you're happy working in the job of your choice. It helps you gain a clear picture of your values and ethics, helping you plan your future – designed by you from the top down.

Although the book is written sequentially, some steps may be more relevant to your current position and you may wish to focus on those first. There is a crossover between steps to reinforce and extract the important elements of your self-discovery, so you can

THE NEXT STEP

revisit the various pages as they become applicable to you and your circumstances.

You're the master of your destiny. The content of this book will help illuminate the path ahead and prompt a clearer direction for self-discovery, growth and implementation to get you closer to your dream practice. Go through the book with an open mind and complete the exercises, exploring what is relevant to you.

THE NEXT STEP

1. JOB SEARCHING

THE NEXT STEP

STEP 1 – Job Searching

There are many ways of searching for work within the Chiropractic profession. There are advertisement boards within colleges, the British Chiropractic Association (BCA), the McTimoney Association (MCA), the Scottish Chiropractic Association (SCA) and the United Chiropractic Association (UCA) magazines and websites. There are also speed meetings hosted by colleges, social media such as Facebook, seminar notice boards and, of course, word of mouth. When you apply for jobs use as many avenues as possible.

It is important to know exactly what you want from a job before accepting an offer – this is further explored in Step 3. On seeing an advertisement that appeals to you, check out the practice's websites before applying for the job to get a feel for their attitude and work environment.

Speak with those who know Chiropractors who work there, especially the associates who currently work there, or the previous associates. If the turnover of associates is high (one or more per year) within a practice, ask them why – to get a true representation of the practice. It may be that they have moved to a more personally fitting practice or it could be it's not a good work environment. Whatever the reason, it is better to hear it from the associate. You will easily find them on the GCC website if they are still based in the UK, or via Facebook. I have discovered in my personal experience, how vital it is to contact these individuals prior to accepting the job, as it can save you a lot of heartache before you sign any contracts.

THE NEXT STEP

Competition

When applying for jobs you will be competing with graduates from other colleges, as well as other Chiropractors who have graduated before you. *Don't let this put you off!* Even if you hear about someone in the years above you are applying for the same job, apply anyway. Hiring is based as much on your personality and how well you'll fit into the practice, as skills. Never let any competition put you off – if you don't try, you'll never know! It's as simple as that.

Jobs

It's a good idea to apply for as many jobs as possible, not only for interview experience but to get a feel for different practices and how they are run. No two interviews will be the same. The more you do, the better picture you will have of what you want and don't want, resulting in greater recognition when the right job comes along.

Chiropractic interviews tend to be atypical of 'industry' interviews where you can do research on the company's five-year plan and infrastructure. They tend to be informal and it's very much a two-way street where you're interviewing the practice as much as they're interviewing you. There are questions in Step 3 on topics you should be thinking about when going through the interview process. Don't be in a rush to secure work (as crazy as that may sound). The one regret many have after leaving college was not taking time out to relax and rejuvenate before starting in practice.

THE NEXT STEP

The truth is, after college, you are saturated emotionally and physically (and chemically with all the 'survival' cortisol, coffee and chocolate). You have just done four to five years of hard graft, putting every ounce of yourself into the degree. You deserve a break to just 'be' – to relax, reset and gain clarity; to start work fresh and be able to give your new patients the very best of you! So don't rush to secure a job.

If you don't start immediately, you will also save financially when you look at the areas discussed in Step 5. At the end of the day, however, the choice is yours. Maybe you're not exhausted and all fired up to get your hands on those patients and start helping them. If so, go for it. I'm simply saying take your time, don't panic and find the job that is right for you.

Clarity

When you apply for work as an associate, try to figure out what you really want in a job. There is such variance in the Chiropractic profession that, realistically, no two practices are the same. There are high volume practices, wellness practices, sports injury practices, paediatric practices, acute care practices, pain relief practices, multi-disciplinary practices, hospital-based practices, rehabilitative practices and gym practices to name but a few. The best thing you can do is answer the questions below, to find out what kind of practice you want to be involved in before exploring the options.

THE NEXT STEP

Usually people start Chiropractic College with an idea of Chiropractic in their heads and hearts, but somewhere along the way, someone (maybe several people) took a fire extinguisher to that flame and reduced it to a mere smoulder, possibly leaving you somewhat confused on how you want to practice as a Chiropractor or even what Chiropractic is.

The following exercises are designed to help you rekindle your version of Chiropractic, so take some time to complete each exercise as they appear.

Exercise 1: Your Chiropractic Vision

Below is an exercise to help you recall why you wanted to become a Chiropractor:

Take a few minutes to think back to your pre-college days and remember the type of Chiropractor you were excited to become upon graduation. Who inspired you? How did they inspire you? What types of patients did you want to see and how did you want to help them? Put the book down, close your eyes and picture it until you're smiling a cheeky grin from the inside...

Having clarified the vision you had of Chiropractic, now take pen to paper and write it down. Write the story of how you were inspired, why you started this journey. Try to remember that 'trigger point', maybe a small thing, that put you on the Chiropractic path. Why did you want to become a chiropractor?

THE NEXT STEP

Exercise 2: Your Ideal Practice Overview

Having gotten a clear picture of how you started your journey, write down answers to the following questions about the practice you see yourself working in:

- What kind of practice do you want to be in?
  High, medium or low volume; wellness, pain-based, rehabilitative, multi-disciplinary? Other?
- How long do you want your treatments/adjustments to be? What are you currently comfortable with? What suits you?
  (The range out there is vast depending on the clinic you enter. You can adjust nine or more people every fifteen minutes, three people every fifteen minutes, one person every fifteen, one person every twenty or one person every thirty to sixty minutes).
- How long do you want to spend with new patients?
  (Again the range is vast – from 20 minutes to 90 minutes). What are you comfortable with?
- How many hours do you want to work per week?
- What would be a good work-life balance for you?
- What techniques do you want to use/develop?
- Who is your ideal patient?
  (Who are the patients you look forward to seeing most? Record why. Are they babies, athletes, elderly, corporate workers? Describe their characteristics. (There's no point in working in a paediatric clinic if you want only to treat adults).

THE NEXT STEP

- What qualities are essential in an ideal practice? (Supportive, helpful, happy, healthy, driven, approachable, indifferent, technique style, multi-disciplinary?)

If you answer these questions honestly, you'll narrow down your search for jobs, saving you time. It is recommended to go for a lot of interviews for the experience and to see the various practices and styles, but this exercise will help you focus on your 'ideal' practice.

You may find you want more time with patients in your first few months of practice, but as your confidence grows, you may need less. Do what suits you and try to match the clinic to your wants/needs. Think of it like a personal relationship; most people have an idea of what they want in a partner, but sometimes it takes a few months to realise it's not working and the best thing to do is end it and move on to something more suitable. The worst thing you can do is stay in the relationship/practice and try to make it work, when you could be happier elsewhere. Your job has to serve you as much as you serve it. You should be happy. Only when you're happy can you serve your patients from the appropriate *place*. If you can get a clear indication of what you want from the offset – you're already off to a winning start!

THE NEXT STEP

STEP 2 – Applying for Jobs

You've seen the advertisements, done your research, and have a clear picture of your ideal practice. But the interview process doesn't start with you shaking the hand of the Principal Chiropractor interviewing you. First comes your CV (curriculum vitae also known as a résumé) and covering letter – so it's crucial to get these right.

NB: From this point forward use a PERSONAL EMAIL ADDRESS – *your college email address is soon to expire!*

Use a professional email address format, e.g.
> [first name].[last name]@gmail.com
> not
> tootsybaby@gmail.com

Can you see the importance of this? Be Professional!

Covering Letter

When applying for a job, the first thing usually requested is a covering letter and your CV. A lot of people are confused about this and unsure of what it's supposed to contain or it's format.

Basically, a covering letter puts flesh on the bones of your CV. It quickly illustrates that you have the qualifications necessary for the job and gives a *personal touch* your CV may lack. A covering letter should be brief and grab the interviewer's attention.

THE NEXT STEP

Letter Format

When formatting your covering letter, you should have your address in the top right-hand corner with your personal email address and phone number underneath, making it easy for them to contact you.

On the left-hand side should be the date, the name of the person to whom you're addressing the letter with their title and surname and their address directly underneath. If you do not know the name of the person, replace it with 'Principal Chiropractor' or 'To whom it may concern', but if possible, always find the name of the person (and spell it correctly!). This may mean contacting the clinic directly, as not all advertisements give the name of the practitioner. This will help your application stand out more than the rest, because you've taken the time to get the appropriate details.

Below the address you should write *Dear* followed by *Dr, Mr, Mrs or Ms,* and their surname; or as stated above: 'Principal Chiropractor'.

Underneath the above you should have a title of what the letter is regarding. For example: **Re: Application for Chiropractic Association Position** or similar. This should be in **bold** to make it stand out. Write your letter, remembering it's going to an office that gets a lot of post daily, and your letter will be opened by a secretary who has to quickly filter all post into categories for distribution to relevant people within a certain time frame.

THE NEXT STEP

The clearer and more distinctive your letter is, with relevant information, the more impressive it will be. You don't get a second chance to make a first impression, so take the time to do it well.

The good news is, once you've done one covering letter, the only information you need to change for other applications are: the recipient's name, the address, the date, and tailor the content to any specific information about their practice – i.e. how you've trained in the technique they use, how you want to work with their type of patient base if they specialise in paediatrics and so forth. It really pays to take the time and do this properly and by adapting your letter to each practice you can make a bigger impression.

Spell check the letter. Use font size 12, Calibri or Garamond (not Times New Roman as it apparently shows a lack of character) with single to 1.5 spacing. The covering letter should be no more than one side of A4 paper. Have someone else read over your letter to check for inconsistencies. Fresh eyes on these things are always helpful, and tools such as Word miss a lot of incorrectly used words (use of an English teacher is great, if you know one!).

Make sure font size and type are consistent throughout and the letter generally looks appealing to the eyes! The following page contains an example of the letter you could write. You can word this how you like, and if you don't like the format, look at other letters you have received to get a wider range of formatting examples. It's always good to stand out from the next person, but make sure it's for the right reasons!

Exercise 3: Create a Covering Letter

Below is an exercise to help you compose your covering letter.

Take some time to gather the necessary content for your covering letter. What information do you deem most important to include in this letter? For example:

- Have you done CPD (Continuing Professional Development) in specific techniques relevant to their practice?
- Do you have interests relevant to their practice?
- Have you started clubs within your college or taken part in team sports?
- Have you been academic rep or been involved in some clubs?
- Have you maintained a job whilst studying?

Write down the main points and then start to formulate it.

THE NEXT STEP

Letter Content

                                                                     First Line of your address
                                                                     Second Line
                                                                     Town
                                                                     County
                                                                     Post Code

                                                                     Email Address
                                                                     Tel Number

[Their reference (If applicable)]

[Dr Healing Hands]
[XYZ Chiropractic Clinic]
[Street]
[Town]
[County, Postcode.]

[Date]

Dear [Dr Healing Hands]

Re: Application for Chiropractic Associate Position

THE NEXT STEP

First paragraph: should start off with what is contained in the envelope: the position you are applying for and how you found out about the job (businesses like to know which sources of advertising are successful), and when you're available to start work.

Example: *Please find enclosed my curriculum vitae for your review for position of Chiropractic Associate, advertised in the [Insert name] Chiropractic Association's magazine. I am a final year student graduating from [name of college] in [month and year].*

Second Paragraph: should summarise your experience to date.

Example: *Over the past year, I have thoroughly enjoyed working with the general public in the [college] clinic. This has been a great experience where I have come across many patients from different walks of life, ages and dispositions with varying complaints, thereby enhancing my clinical experience.*

Next paragraph(s): should summarise your strengths and how they might be an advantage to their practice. Give them a brief synopsis of any extra-curricular activities in which you have participated (these paragraphs are differentiating you from your fellow applicants and can spark light bulb moments in your interviewer's head, so hit the key points here – make them want to read your CV).

THE NEXT STEP

Example: *Currently I predominantly practise diversified technique and enjoy incorporating my skills in soft tissue manipulation. I also devise and implement rehabilitation exercises when appropriate.*

I have partaken in many CPD courses inclusive of [example], [example] and many others. I do intend to continue my CPD development to expand my scope of skills so I can best serve the public.

During my college years, I have also maintained the position of [example] and worked part time as a [example]. This has enabled me to time manage efficiently, grow as a practitioner and communicate effectively at many different levels.

Last Paragraph: should mention you're available for interview and/or observations, thank the interviewer and say you look forward to hearing from them soon.

Example: *I would be grateful for the opportunity to come and observe you at your clinic and meet the rest of the team at your convenience.*

I look forward to hearing from you soon.

THE NEXT STEP

You should end the letter with: 'Yours sincerely', and below that, your full name with enough space between the last line and your name for your signature.

Yours sincerely

[*Your signature*]
[John Smith]

Next is an example of what the page might look like. You may find yours flows onto a second page. That's fine but don't go beyond two pages.

THE NEXT STEP

                                                  1 Second Drive
                                                  The Heath
                                                  Reading
                                                  Berkshire BE1 2AB

                                                  myname@bt.com
                                                  07812 345 678

Your Ref: ABC/0011

Dr Healing Hands
XYZ Chiropractic Clinic
First Street
Big Town
Kent, AB12 3CD

Date 01/01/2017

Dear Dr Healing Hands

Re: Application for Chiropractic Associate Position

Please find enclosed my curriculum vitae for your review for position of Chiropractic Associate, advertised in the [Insert name] Chiropractic Association's magazine.

I am a final year student graduating from [name of college] in [month and year].

Over the past year, I have thoroughly enjoyed working with the general public in the [college] clinic. This has been a great experience where I have come across many patients from different walks of life, ages and dispositions with varying complaints, thereby enhancing my clinical experience.

Currently I predominantly practise diversified technique and enjoy incorporating my skills in soft tissue manipulation. I also devise and implement rehabilitation exercises when appropriate.

Example layout of a Covering Letter (page 1)

THE NEXT STEP

I have partaken in many CPD courses inclusive of [example], [example] and many others. I do intend to continue my CPD development to expand my scope of skills so I can best serve the public.

During my College years, I have also maintained the position of [example] and worked part time as a [example]. This has enabled me to time manage efficiently, grow as a practitioner and communicate effectively at many different levels.

I would be grateful for the opportunity to come and observe you at your clinic and meet the rest of the team at your convenience.

I look forward to hearing from you soon.

Yours sincerely

John Smith
John Smith

Example layout of a Covering Letter (page 2)

Curriculum Vitae (CV)

A curriculum vitae (CV) also known as a résumé, provides an overview of a person's experience and other qualifications. It is usually a **maximum** of two sides of A4 paper, and therefore contains only a summary of your employment history, qualifications, education, and some personal information.

A CV should be updated to change the emphasis of the information depending on the job you are applying for. Below is a recommended format for a CV following much research in different areas and speaking to many people in Human Resources for the best format. Again, this can be personal preference and Google supplies many examples. Do what works for you! Remember with your CV, you want to give them enough information to cover the essentials, but leave enough curiosity to require further information during the interview.

Format and Content of CV

Page One
The first page should contain your main **contact information**: Full name, telephone number(s), and email address. Make sure you fill in your personal email address, as you will lose access to the college one when you leave. Also, many times I have found college servers can be down at weekends inhibiting access when you most need it.

Your CV should contain a brief **personal profile**. This is a good way to express your personality, and makes you distinct from others. It's a brief overview of your qualities. It can be difficult to describe

THE NEXT STEP

yourself positively (as humans, we tend to see the negative before the positive), therefore ask tutors/staff/friends/family, 'how would you describe me?' You may be happily surprised with the words they use; a description that you may never have thought of yourself. When I asked tutors, a common word among them was 'diligent' – I personally would not have thought of this myself therefore this proved a very useful exercise! Ask as many people as possible, and <u>write the replies down</u>, it's easy to forget. You're not going to use all of them, but you'll start to notice the more people you ask, the more words will become repeated and take that as an obvious trait. Then turn these into three to four sentences and your profile is done.

Your **education** should be summarised on the first page and contain the years you studied, where and what you studied. CPD is a LOT cheaper for students to participate in; therefore, make use of the different courses available. Remember you want to stand out from your fellow applicants, so this is a great way to bring skill to the practice you're going to work. Think about it, the more tools you have in your toolbox, the more useful you're going to be for the job. The CPD section should contain the date, what the CPD was, who the CPD was with and the amount of hours CPD completed.

Page Two
The second page should contain a summary of your **employment**, outlining dates, where and what you did (relevant to the position you are applying). This should be in chronological order starting with the most recent.

THE NEXT STEP

It should contain your **achievements** to date and any awards you have received, outlining the year and the achievement details.

The next section contains your **interests**, which is best summarised in sentence format. This should be examples of spending time on your own as well as group activities that you have participated in. Outlining both demonstrates the ability to be good on your own as well as part of a team. Mention any competitions you've been involved in. Don't lie about this (or anything else in your CV) in case your interviewer enjoys the same activities you've listed and initiates a conversation about it – that would be embarrassing and worse than that, it would undermine you and your CV.

The last section is for your **references**. A lot of people write in the name, address and contact number of someone who will act as a reference. I personally write 'available on request' beside this section. If the Principal Chiropractor wants a reference, I prefer they contact me first – this is a personal thing. This has been accepted with every job I have ever applied for, in and outside Chiropractic.

Remember it is **maximum 2 pages**, not minimum, so if you went straight to college from A-levels and have done zero CPD courses whilst at college, then your CV will have less content. It is simply a matter of merging the two pages together but keep font 10 – 12 pt.

THE NEXT STEP

CV Checklist:

When you prepare your CV, ensure it is:
- 2 Pages max (font size no smaller than 10pt)
- Spell checked!!!!! (Don't rely on your word spellcheck alone, they often miss correctly spelt words used incorrectly such as <u>their</u> instead of <u>there</u>).
- In chronological order of <u>most recent</u> in all sections.
- Positive – what makes you different?
- Consistent format. Capital letters in the correct places. Bold/italic in the correct places. Dates in the same format. Be consistent and pay attention to detail!

If you are sending your CV and covering letter electronically, convert the word document to PDF and save a copy in a folder in case you need the details for future reference.

QUESTION:
Would *you* interview you after reading your covering letter and CV?

THE NEXT STEP

Exercise 4: Create a CV

Write a summary for the content of your CV. Answer the questions below to start.

QUESTIONS:
- What contact information will you use?
- How would your personal profile describe you?
- Where have you previously studied? What CPD have you done?
- Who have you previously worked for?
- What are your interests? What do you like to do?
- Who is the best person to give you a character reference?

Now take the time to systematically place the above content on one or two pages. Example in the following pages.

THE NEXT STEP

CV Example

Page one

Name: Jo Bloggs	**Address:** Line 1
Tel no: 000 0000 0000	Line 2
Email: me@yahoo.com	Town
	County
	Postcode

PROFILE:
Brief description (3-4 lines) of your attributes in sentence format.

EDUCATION:

YY – Present (Graduate MM/YY)	**Name and address of Chiropractic College** Degree Title
YY – YY	**Name and address of College** Qualification achieved e.g. Diploma in Massage/Business Studies.
YY – YY	**Name and address of School attended** Subjects and Grades achieved e.g. Spanish (A), English (B) etc.

CPD Courses Completed alongside [Course]:

MM YY	CPD Event with [Organisation/Person]	XX CPD hours
MM YY	CPD Event with [Organisation/Person]	XX CPD hours
	e.g. SOT Module 1 with SOTO EUROPE	*12 CPD hours*

Page two

EMPLOYMENT:	
MM[1] YY[2] – MM YY	**Job Title, Organisation, County, Country**
	Brief job description of main significant tasks.
MM YY – MM YY	**Job Title, Organisation, County, Country**
	Brief job description of main significant tasks.
MM YY – MM YY	**Job Title, Organisation, County, Country**
	Brief job description of main significant tasks.
ACHIEVEMENTS:	
YY-YY	Achievement accomplished
YY-YY	Achievement accomplished
YY-YY	Achievement accomplished
INTERESTS:	
Brief summary of activities you enjoy e.g. running, athletics, horse riding, socialising. (In sentence format)	
REFERENCES:	
'Available on request' OR: name, address, phone number and position held, if preferred.	

---

[1] MM – Month in figures e.g. '06' for June
[2] YY – Year in figures e.g. '12' for 2012

3 INTERVIEW PROCESS

STEP 3 – Interview Process

Preparing for the interview

Congratulations, you have sent off your CV and covering letter and potentially have had a response by email, phone call or letter inviting you for an interview/observations. If you have not received contact within 2 weeks of sending off your application, follow this up with a polite phone call to the practice. State that you sent your application for the post advertised in [source] on X date and you're just calling to confirm they received the application and are enquiring as to what stage the interview process is at, because you haven't heard anything yet. This phone call should be received nicely and they should inform you with a date to get back to you. Don't sit and wonder.

So, what now? (apart from being excited and nervous all at the same time). First thing you do is check out their website again, get a feel for the place. Would you want to be a patient there based on the website? If so, why? If not – why not?

When attending an interview, you will be assessed from the moment you arrive: by the receptionist, the Principal Chiropractor, and anyone else you talk to, i.e. patients (they're usually asked for feedback).

Clothes

Be organised on what you're going to wear: shirt and tie for male, blouse for female and trousers for both. Women should not wear a skirt in case they are required to carry out an adjustment. Smart shoes (no stiletto heels, ladies) and hair tied back if it is long. You want to look professional, clean, tidy and presentable.

Plan your Journey

Research how long it will take you to get to the practice and always allow for traffic congestion. Usually the areas of job application are not around the corner and can take several hours to get to by train, bus or car, so know your journey. Lateness will not be the best impression to give. If by some chance, traffic is a nightmare and you can't see yourself arriving on time, call the practice and inform them of the distance left and your predicament.

Write down the practice contact details and bring them with you! Don't depend on electronics in case you don't have a mobile signal, and as silly and obvious as it may sound, ensure your phone is fully charged and bring a phone charger as there's nothing worse than your phone dying when you need it!

On Arrival

On arrival at the practice, make yourself known to the receptionist and the reason for your visit. Don't assume they know who you are and why you're there. They may still have practice running if there are other Chiropractors/therapists working. Remember you want to help people as much as possible – they have enough going on in their own lives/working days.

THE NEXT STEP

Awaiting Interview

When you've confirmed your arrival, if they tell you to take a seat in the reception, observe how reception works. Notice what you like about the place. What literature do they have? How are patients being received and processed? What's the atmosphere like? What's the feel of the place? What smells, sights, sounds etc. can you notice? DO NOT EVEN THINK about taking out your phone: it's on silent, off vibrate and out of sight because, cleverly, you did all this before entering the building.

Sit confidently, relax and take it all in. Chat to the front desk staff if they are not busy. Do you like this place so far? Remember you're being assessed by everyone as soon as you walk through the door and they'll be asked for an opinion. If you sit slouched, picking your nose (again, you'd be surprised) or on your phone – would you hire you?

You're likely to be nervous; that's normal, but try to be confident in your answers and adjustments (yes, some Chiropractors want to feel your palpation/technique skills). Don't panic if you don't get an audible release, technique is something that can be developed, and the Principal Chiropractor is getting a feel for you more than the end result (plus they may have just been adjusted!). Be present, be yourself, confident in your years of training, and do your best. That, realistically, is all you can do!

During interviews, you may come across some strong characters. Don't feel bullied! There's a lot of opinion out there about technique, chiropractic and politics. Some people can take it too far. Just stay authentic to you. If you find you're on the defensive during the interview process, it may be that the practice isn't right for you; and if you were to work there, over time, it may erode your confidence in what you feel is right. Be very aware of this and always go with your gut feeling.

Observation

If you get the opportunity to observe in the practice, ask to also observe the other associates or chat to them. Most interviews are quite relaxed and it's important that you get a proper feel for the environment and colleagues. Observe for two hours minimum from all aspects: patient handling, reception handling, transfer of patients from reception to rooms and back to reception. Notice the equipment in the room, the technique used, the interaction between doctor and patient. Can you see yourself working this way? Will you be working from the same room or a different one? If different – go and check it out – can you see yourself working there? Does it feel good or do you have reservations? Are you excited or doubtful? If so why? Acknowledge this.

As stated above, if you're leaving an interview not feeling good about yourself or the practice, this is not a reflection on you – it simply illustrates it's not the place to begin your career. Always be true to yourself and find a practice with people you are comfortable with. This is why it is important to do the exercises within this book and have a clear picture of who you are and how you want to practice.

THE NEXT STEP

On the other hand, if you're leaving the interview, hopeful, excited and wanting to work there as soon as possible – acknowledge what it is about the practice and people that make you feel this way.

After each interview, reflect on the process and answer the questions in Exercise 5.

Remember: you're interviewing them as much as they're interviewing you! This is going to be your future, as temporary or as long as the position may be for. The objective is to get off to a good start instead of 'baptism by fire' like many new graduates have experienced.

If baptism by fire does happen to you, know that it's temporary and 'this too shall pass'. By making a different decision and taking action on this decision, you get a different outcome. You can start again elsewhere as simply as you started there!

Exercise 5: Interview Questions

This exercise contains a series of questions to potentially ask during your interview. You don't have to learn them off by heart or take the page in with you. They should naturally unfold through conversation. These questions are a more detailed follow on version from Exercise 2 in Step 1 with some overlap.

THE NEXT STEP

It would be a good idea to go through each question and answer them for yourself, to know exactly what you want in a practice. The clearer the picture you have in your head of the ideal practice for you, the easier it will be to filter what you want from what you don't want.

QUESTIONS:
- What type of practice is it?
- How long are treatment times? New patient times? Report of findings times?
- Do you have a patient base to take over from?
- How many associates in clinic?
- How are new patients distributed?
- What promotional work do they do? And what are you expected to do (if anything)?
- What are the opening hours of the practice?
- What will be your hours of work?
- If there are no patients during the working day, can you leave?
- If you go on holiday/take time off:
    - Do they see your patients or do you have to supply a locum?
    - Is there a cap on the amount of holiday you can take or the length of holiday?
- If they go on holiday/take time off:
    - Do you see their patients?
    - Do you get a capped fee or percentage per head?

THE NEXT STEP

- Will you be employed/self-employed?
  - If employed, after x amount do you get a percentage? What are the terms of that employment: do they pay your GCC, Association fee and CPD? And if they pay these, what happens if you leave early? Are they deducted from your percentage throughout the year? Will they contribute to the pension scheme?
  - If self-employed, does your percentage increase after a certain time?
  - Do they have a contract to clarify the agreement?
- Have they ever had an associate before?
  - How long did the associate work there? Get details, and contact them to find out why they left and what it was like to work in the practice [this is a must – make sure their history doesn't affect your future!!!]
- Are you expected to be part of a particular Association?
- What equipment do they use? Do they have X-ray facilities? Posture scanner, balance scales? EMG scans? other?
- What kind of benches do they have?
- Are activators etc. supplied or do you use your own kit? Models? Books etc.
- Are you expected to use a specific technique or can you do your own thing? (And does that still apply if you're covering their patients?)
- Are patients gowned/clothed?
- Are records electronic/paper?

- What options are available for getting paid: daily/weekly/monthly?
- Do you get paid in cash/cheque/bank transfer?
- What percentage do you get? (ranges 35-55%)
- Is there any other money taken out of your percentage for stationery, receptionist, advertising etc.? Or do you get the full percentage?
- What support/training do you get?

Exercise 6: Extra Interview Questions

Can you think of any other questions to ask during the interview that may be personal to you? If so, write them down. Prepare for the interview and get as much out of them as possible. Only then can you make an INFORMED decision.

If you get offered the job there and then, congratulations! But make sure you take some time to 'think about it' – up to a week if this is possible, especially when you are doing other interviews. You want to find the best place that suits you. They may also have other interviews to complete and may have to get back to you with a decision. Before you leave, agree a date when you will let each other know if you're going to be a future associate of that practice.

THE NEXT STEP

Post Interview Questions

Once you have completed the interview, it may be good to sit, reflect and answer some questions before the next one. When you come out of an interview, go to a quiet area (local park, café or pub) and record the answers to the questions in Exercises 5 and 6 (because they'll get muddied in your memory with other interviews over time) and those below entitled 'post interview questions'. If you do this each time, on completion of all interviews, you'll have a ranking system of preferred jobs.

QUESTIONS:
- Do you like the area?
- Can you see yourself living/working there? Why?
- Do you like the clinic and how they operate? What do you like?
- Do you like the Principal Chiropractor? The team? What do you like about them?
- Did you feel energised or drained when in the environment?
- Do they have the same philosophy as you?
- Is it financially viable?
- Will this practice help you grow personally, professionally and authentically?

The Area

Choosing an area to live can be a challenging decision. Should you pick an area where you're most likely to succeed, or choose where you will have emotional support? Should you be close to family and friends, or are you happy to know no one to begin with?

When going for interviews, it's not only about the practice you're going to be working in, it's also about what you're going to spend your time doing outside of work. If you have moved to a place you don't know, you can become somewhat isolated therefore you may like some 'comforts' within reach.

In the area you've just had the interview, talk to the local people in parks, cafés and pubs and ask them their opinions of the neighbourhood. If you like the practice, revisit the area on another day to get a feel for it and research the following to get an overview of what will be involved in moving there.

Exercise 7: Your Ideal Area

Before embarking on interviews, take a few minutes to establish the kind of place you would like to live. Answer the following questions to gain insight.

THE NEXT STEP

QUESTIONS:
- How much does it cost to live there? What are the prices of housing, council tax etc.?
- What amenities are present? How close are they?
- What clubs/interests are there?
- If you go at school finishing time – what are the kids/parents like?
- What social life is there?
- What necessities do you require to live in an area – 24-hour shop, proximity to public transport, airports, countryside?

THE NEXT STEP

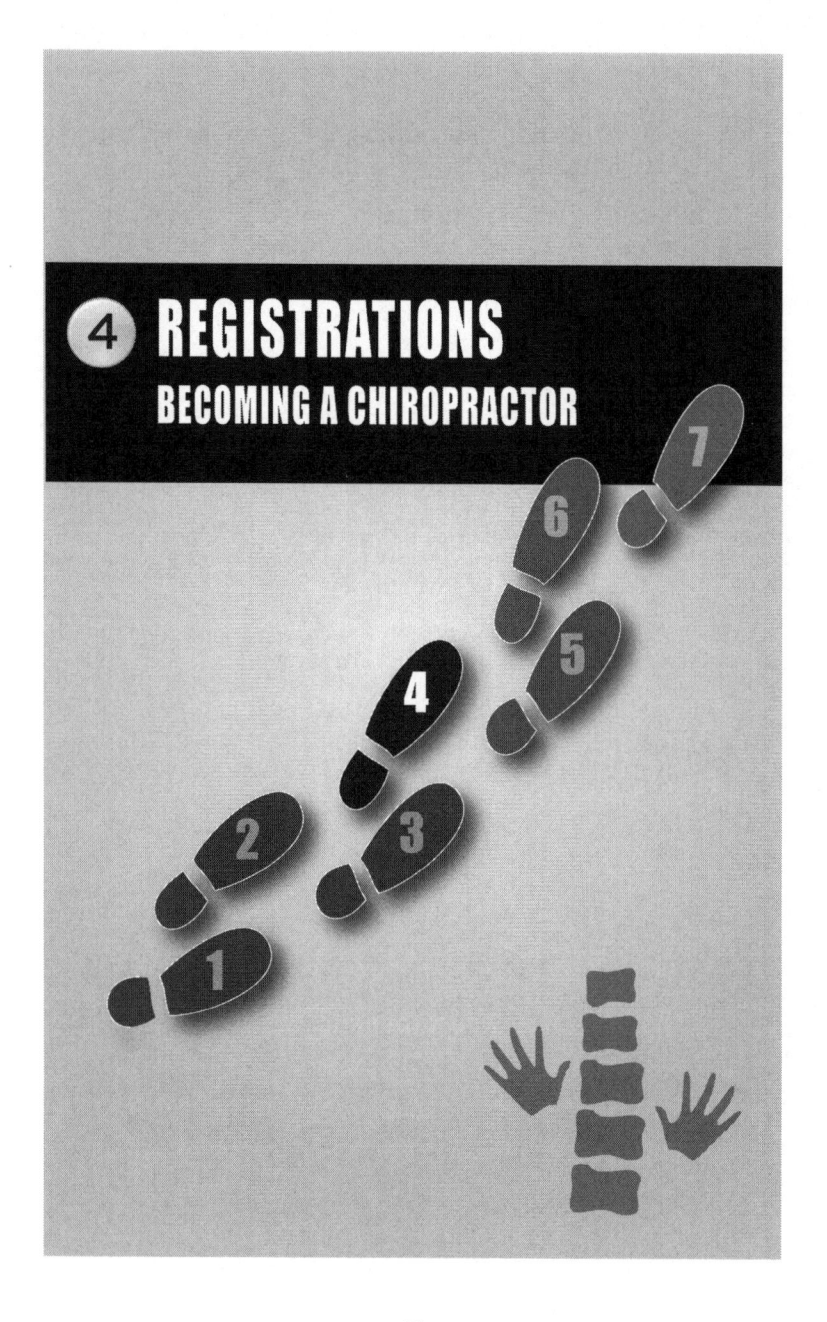

4. REGISTRATIONS
BECOMING A CHIROPRACTOR

STEP 4 – Registrations

You have gone through the application and interview process and you have secured your first job – *congratulations!* Now it's time to prepare yourself for the graduate world as an associate Chiropractor, if this is the option you have chosen.

If you're someone who has decided to open your own practice straight away, this step is still relevant to you, so don't miss out on the fundamental information given on the necessities to becoming a Doctor of Chiropractic.

Before you get started there are several registrations you must complete before you can work with patients as a Chiropractor. These are:

Compulsory:
- Insurance Company
- General Chiropractic Council (GCC)

Also, if you are becoming self-employed:
- HMRC
- Bank

Optional:
- Chiropractic Association (BCA / MCA / SCA / UCA)
- Royal College of Chiropractors
- European Chiropractic Union (ECU)

And if you are becoming self-employed:
- Accountant

THE NEXT STEP

Chiropractic Associations

Remember: your contact details on these forms should remain accessible over the next few months, e.g. permanent address, personal email address and mobile (not college info).

Upon graduation there is a certain order in which things are best done. If you are going to join an Association, it is best to register with them first as there can be many benefits attached to membership, like a reduction in fee with the insurance company. Though it is not compulsory to join an Association, it is better practice to have a team of experienced people behind you when you run into unfamiliar territory.

Before you join an Association, consider the following:
- Membership fee from graduation date and annual fee thereafter.
- Insurance companies linked to that Association (fee, stipulations, amount covered, and run-off cover should you change insurance provider).
- Membership stipulations – do you have to complete the PRT (Post-Registration Training) programme and are there any other stipulations required?
- What if you want to leave the Association? How does this effect your insurance and are there any other effects that may occur?
- What support is offered for legal, personal, business, mentorship?

THE NEXT STEP

- What literature is available for Chiropractors, patients, advertising and so on (what is free and what is discounted as a member?)
- What discounts and offers is the association connected with? E.g. card machines, insurance companies, equipment?
- What guidelines are available for various aspects of Chiropractic: law, business, X-rays and the like?
- Philosophy – do their values coincide with yours?

Check out all the entitlements and benefits of each association before deciding. Check out which ones are free and for how long post-graduation? Investigate their websites and explore which association suits you best.

Remember you are investing three figured amounts annually to this organisation, make sure it is one that serves you and your needs the best! Don't only look at how the Association meets your needs currently, think about when you are more experienced and potentially opening up your own practice.

Choosing your Association is important, so take the time to compare, contrast and apply to your individual case. Ask whatever questions necessary of them and make an informed decision before taking out full membership. Ask Chiropractors which Association they are with and why did they choose that Association? Have they been with any of the other Associations? If so, why did they change? How have they found their experiences with each Association?

THE NEXT STEP

As the American author Brendan Burchard says 'It's hard to have a vision for your life if you've never seen anything – get into the world. Explore'. Choosing an Association is about you and your needs, not what your friends are doing. Don't be misguided by someone else's opinion and wants. What do YOU need, as a graduate and who do you need behind you in the future? ... Then choose!

Exercise 8: Association Exploration

Without looking at the various Association sites, first think of what it is you require from an Association. This is something you may not have contemplated before and it's good to explore an unknown territory before committing to an Association.

QUESTIONS:
- What do you want from an Association?
- What do you expect your Association to do for you?
- In what areas do you expect them to support you and how?
- What benefits do you want from an Association?
- What documents do you expect to have access to with your Association?

THE NEXT STEP

Chiropractic Insurance

As of **17 July 2015,** the minimum amount of cover held under an indemnity insurance policy must be **£5million** when practising as a chiropractor.

On top of professional indemnity, you **MUST** have public liability and product liability (This should automatically be included in your chiropractic policy but always check). If you have employees, contractors, casual workers or temporary staff, you also must have employer's liability insurance.

The GCC stated in their COPSOP 2010 that 'you are personally liable to individual patients for any assessment or care you provide' and 'personal liability applies to all Chiropractors, including those working as a locum, those working in a practice run by a principal, and those working for a limited company'.

If your circumstances change in any way that could affect your policy, it is vital to inform the insurance company immediately. The GCC state you are legally required to have 'enough run-off cover to protect you for the period you were in practice'.

Upon graduation, insurance is usually discounted depending on the Association you have joined and each Association has a different insurance company linked to it. It is worth investigating with the different Associations, how the insurance works and taking the policy that best suits your needs.

THE NEXT STEP

Be aware, if you are taking an insurance policy in conjunction with Association membership and you decide to leave your current Association, it may affect the validity of your current insurance policy. You **must** check the terms and conditions of the insurance policy and Association and how they integrate/affect each other.

Exercise 9: Insurance Cover

Answer the questions below to gain an insight into the various insurance companies available and what is required with each.

QUESTIONS:
- Who are the various insurance companies that cover Chiropractic?
- What discount or terms and conditions do they have with/without Association membership?
- What does the insurance cover?

THE NEXT STEP

General Chiropractic Council (GCC)

Remember: your contact details being completed on these forms should be accessible over the next few months i.e. permanent address, personal email address and mobile (not College info).

The next organisation you **MUST** register with is the General Chiropractic Council (GCC) if you want to work as a Chiropractor in the UK. The GCC was created by an Act of Parliament (The Chiropractor's Act 1994) and has held a register of Chiropractors since 1999.

The role of the GCC is to:
- Protect patients
- Set standards of education
- Set standards in conduct and practice for registered Chiropractors

Application to the GCC involves downloading the application form from the registration section of the GCC website (www.gcc-uk.org) and completing the many stipulations to process the application.

It is important to note the registration fee is the same at whatever point in the year you join. There is no provision under the GCC rules to allow for pro-rata payments.

THE NEXT STEP

Upon graduation in July, if you are going to practise as a Chiropractor within the UK straight away (or in August, September, October of year of graduation), you must pay a fee of £750 or £100 if you are not practising. The retention fee of £800 is then due at the end of November (several months later) for registration in advance for the following year.

If you do not register until after 10 November, you effectively get 13 months for the price of 12 however you CANNOT practise as a Chiropractor until you receive the registration number from the GCC. You must double check this with the GCC in case they have changed their terms since the time of writing this.

The GCC registration year is from 01 January to 31 December. The GCC will not accept your application unless you have your certificate of insurance for professional indemnity of a minimum of £5 million.

To complete the application, you will also need:
(Please ensure you check the GCC website www.gcc-uk.org for updated information)
- A completed **application form** downloadable from the GCC website.
- **Registration fee**. Note, if you send a cheque it can take up to five working days to clear (check with your bank, some do fast clearance now as standard).
- Evidence of your **Chiropractic qualification** – which is a certificate/confirmation letter issued by the college you graduated from as recognised by the GCC.

THE NEXT STEP

- A **character reference** dated <u>within 3 months</u> of the date of the letter, so make sure you do not wait too long to send this off. They also stipulate it must be written by a professional person. *Ensure the person writes their qualifications and profession below their name and signature –* <u>*or it will not be accepted*</u>*!*
- A **medical report** from a doctor to say you are fit to practise. You MUST have been registered with your GP for a <u>minimum of 4 years</u> and usually doctors charge up to £50 for this letter. The <u>original copy</u> must be sent to the GCC. Print out the 'information note for your General Practitioner' from the GCC website and attach it to your request (with all your up-to-date personal details) for your GP. On collection of the letter, before you leave the surgery, check all the information is correct as you can be waiting up to 3 weeks for a GP letter of this kind and the GCC will not accept errors.
- If you have not been registered with the GP for 4+ years, the GCC will accept a medical report from a GP based on medical examination. Note this examination and report will have a fee as set out by the medical practice.
- **Certified copy of passport** and any other change of name documents (ensure it is certified by either the person who has written your character reference, or a college official where you obtained your qualification including the formal stamp of the college).
The certifier must write 'I confirm this to be a true and accurate copy of the original passport as sighted by me' followed by their name and signature.

THE NEXT STEP

- Evidence of your **professional indemnity insurance to** practise in the UK. This is the front cover that states the policy number, your name and address and the amount you are covered for (minimum £5 million) with the policy start date. Note the policy start date is not the date you <u>intend</u> to start to practise, as the GCC cannot process your application until the policy <u>has started</u>, so start your policy with immediate effect. It does not cost any extra.

You may also be asked for the following if it apples to you:
- **Certificates of good standing and certificates of current professional status** from any regulatory bodies with whom you are or have been registered.
- **Police record check**, only if you have a criminal record.

Ensure you check the GCC website for updated information as the above stipulations may change as the GCC evolves.

Exercise 10: GCC Requirements

Before applying for GCC registration, complete the points below so you know where your gaps are:
- Make a list of the documents required by the GCC
- What documents do you already have?
- What documents do you need?
- Who do you need to talk to about the outstanding documents/certificates/ references/reports?
- Put deadlines/dates to request, receive and process these documents into a calendar.

THE NEXT STEP

All correspondence from the GCC is usually sent to your registered *practice* address and not to your home address. It is important to keep this information up to date on the GCC website should you move practices in the future – this can be done online when you receive your login details.

Before sending any of the documents to the GCC, check they meet the criteria stipulated, EXACTLY how it is stipulated. If the GP registration of four years is even short by a few months, the letter may not be accepted. If the character reference does not have a date on it or state how long they have known you, it may not be accepted. They may also not accept an amended copy, and request a new reference from someone else. *Ensure you photocopy all documents before sending for your records.*

Allow time for the GCC to process the application. Check with the GCC how long it will take to process your application, but until you have a registration number from them (and all criteria is met fully with no other 'errands to run' to meet their conditions), you are not allowed to treat patients as a Chiropractor and your insurance will not cover you; plus it is a criminal offence to practise Chiropractic without being registered Make sure everything is tight, ticked, dotted and crossed before you submit the paper work! Be diligent and assume hassle!

THE NEXT STEP

TIPS:

1. On the back of the GCC application form, there is a direct debit form. As convenient as this is to complete, if you do not have the money in the bank account when they take it out in November, you will run into bank charges. There is nothing worse than going to your bank account thinking you have a couple of hundred in there to discover that you are in deficit and pending a £40 overdraft fine. To prevent this, I didn't complete the direct debit form. The GCC then prompt for the payment of £800 to retain the registration for the following year.
2. Get a receipt for the letter from your GP and you can claim this against tax. You can also claim the price of the envelope and stamp and petrol to collect the letter etc. As Tesco says, 'every little helps'.
3. Do not register with the Associations, GCC or insurance company before you get your exam results confirming you have passed the degree and are now officially a 'Doctor of Chiropractic'. Have everything ready to send upon receipt of your results; and then have the delight of posting those envelopes!
4. When posting all the documentation to the relevant places (GCC, Association etc.), send all envelopes by registered post. Although more expensive, it means they are traceable. Call each organisation a couple of days later to confirm they have received the documents, and request a processing time.

Royal College of Chiropractors (RCoC)

The Royal College of Chiropractors offer a postgraduate training programme to allow a smoother transition from graduation into the profession. It involves having a mentor and completing a series of academic tasks. To do this, you must register with the RCoC, however the Post Registration Training (PRT) programme is optional and not a pre-requisite of all the Associations or the GCC. Further information is available on www.rcc-uk.org/prt

Exercise 11: PRT Programme

Can you answer all the questions below? If not, get in contact with the appropriate organisations to gain the answers.

QUESTIONS:
- Does your Association require you to complete the PRT programme?
- What do you need to put in place to partake in the programme?
- Who will be your mentor during the programme?
- What is involved in completing the programme?

European Chiropractors' Union (ECU)

According to their website, The European Chiropractors' Union (ECU) is established to promote the development of Chiropractic in Europe as well as to pursue the interests of Chiropractic as a science and a profession by research, teaching, publications and legal activities. It represents the Chiropractic profession in Europe on a 'supranational level'. Benefits of joining the ECU, their fees and further information can be found on their website www.chiropractic-ecu.org.

HMRC (If becoming self-employed)

Upon graduation you must choose whether you are going to become employed or self-employed, as the practice where you start work may require you to become one or the other. If you decide to be self-employed (known as a 'sole trader') you MUST register with HMRC within **3 months** of starting work or you can face a fine of £100. On completion of registration you should receive a 10-digit Unique Tax Registration (UTR) number which is necessary for completing the self-assessment[3] (whether it be completed by you or your accountant). To register, you must complete the CWF1 form or to do it online at www.hmrc.gov.uk. Remember to save a screenshot of the completed registration as proof.

Exercise 12: HMRC Registration

Answer the questions below to gain necessary information prior to registration with HMRC.

QUESTIONS:
- Who did I last work for? Who do I need to contact to get my P45?
- What address am I registering my self-employment to?

---

[3] Self-assessment is also known as a tax return

THE NEXT STEP

- What information do I need to register (National Insurance number etc.)
- What follow-up do I require to ensure everything is in place?
- What information do I need to complete registration (HMRC website, HMRC contact number etc.)

Bank

When you are self-employed, it is important to have a new bank account from the beginning. People think you have to have a 'business account' if you are self-employed, but if you are a sole trader (not a limited company), according to Martin Lewis from Money Saving Expert, you can simply use a personal bank account for your business. You **must** however check your terms and conditions as some banks won't allow this. Some banks also offer 12–18 months' free business banking.

There are many charges associated with a 'business account', and each bank, of course, is different. Charges of up to £25 are possible, on top of monthly account fees as well as being charged for depositing cash/cheques. Personal bank accounts are usually fees-free if you're in credit. You can also get an overdraft allowance for a personal account. With the personal account you can also get a cheque book and debit card.

It is important to have a separate account for your business to make book-keeping easy. It is also completely separate from your private account, making it much easier if HMRC need do an in-depth enquiry into your tax affairs. This account should be used ONLY for business purposes so have all your business-orientated income/expenses going in/out of this account.

Exercise 13: Bank Registration

Below is a list of questions worth answering prior to deciding which bank account you're going to open.

QUESTIONS:
- Which bank(s) am I going to open the necessary accounts with?
- What are the requirements to open the accounts: e.g. a certain income per calendar month, existing account, other?
- What documents do I need to open these accounts (passport, proof of address, other)?
- What will these accounts be used for?
- Do these accounts give me the facilities I need: e.g. online banking, debit card, cheque book etc.?
- What are the terms and conditions of each account?

THE NEXT STEP

Accountant

If you become self-employed, you can do your own accounts, but in general, hiring an accountant, especially when setting yourself up, can actually save you money overall. So where does one start when searching for one? I guess it's quite similar to any other profession: you have advertisements in the local directories, adverts on the TV, and there are offices often in the high street. But the best way, by far, is by word of mouth.

Ask people with small businesses who they use. How long have they been using their accountant? How much do they charge for services? And does the accountant save them on their tax bill via expenses?

If you've just moved to an unfamiliar area, research by asking other local professionals/self-employed people, who they use. When you have gathered a few names, call those recommended accountants and ask for a FREE consultation to discuss how you are going to work together. Be sure to establish upfront that it's a free consultation, as the last thing you want to be landed with is an unexpected bill. Of course, your accountant does not have to be local to you.

During my consultation, I asked so many basic questions that each accountant probably thought I didn't even graduate! We trained in Chiropractic, not accountancy. Everything in this life is learned, it is not automatic. Never be afraid to ask questions and get educated. A good accountant will educate you.

THE NEXT STEP

QUESTIONS:

I asked things like:
- At what time of year is the tax paid?
- How much should I be putting away out of my earnings?
- Do I need a separate bank account (as discussed previously)?
- What is the best way of monitoring what I spend?
- How do I keep my receipts?
- Can I use different accounts if I don't have the business card with me?
- How much do I pay myself?
- By what date do I have to submit my workings?
- Do I need to fill in the self-assessment form or do they do it?
- What do I need for the self-assessment form?
- What things fall into the expenses category?
- How does payment of the student loan work?
- How much do they charge and what does that entail?
- Is there a monthly payment scheme in place for fees?
- Do they have a system for me to enter the data onto?

I 'interviewed' six accountants before I made my decision. The prices ranged from £200 to £1,600! Accountants vary in price depending on what is required. A simple tax return can be as little as £150 so shop around and do the appropriate research.

THE NEXT STEP

The accountant I chose was the only accountant to ask me if I had my 'UTR'. As explained earlier, the UTR (Unique Taxpayer Reference) is a code that HMRC give you to enable you to submit your tax return which will only be issued on receipt of your P45. He explained that if I didn't have this code, then when my tax return was due, I would have to go through some delayed palaver with administration, tracking, posting etc. and I could suffer a nasty fine for not having submitted the tax return on time!

It's these little things that result in the challenging situations that should be avoided. So, if any of you have been in employment during your 4/5+ years of study, get your P45 from your last employer and send it to HMRC and follow up with a request for the UTR. HMRC will not automatically send it to you, nor will they chase you for it! Welcome to the world of responsibility!

On starting out as a new graduate and a self-employed Chiropractor, everything is new. Can I claim back buying a bin for the office as a business expense? Or when using my car – can I claim back petrol used, or its servicing? What about when I did CPD and had to buy food – was that a claimable expense?

It was becoming overwhelmed in a state of confusion which lead to my first call to an accountant. He said, in one line, what defined an expense: 'Anything that is used wholly and exclusively for the business is an expense'.

THE NEXT STEP

So the bin was put on the business card, as was the CPD and food, because I wouldn't be at the seminar if the practice didn't require it. The car wasn't as straightforward because it was not a company vehicle, however there are allowances for such things. For further information and some clarity, HMRC have outlined clearly what can and cannot be classified as an expense on their website: www.hmrc.gov.uk, but if you have any confusion or queries about this, discuss it with your accountant. Ensure you do not get charged extra from the accountant to consult them on queries.

Exercise 14: Accountant Questions

Before choosing an accountant answer the questions below to get a clear picture of what you want from an accountant.

QUESTIONS:
- What do I want from an accountant?
- Who do I know who has an accountant?
- What am I willing to pay an accountant?
- How will I organise my finances?
- What do I need to understand to become self-employed and manage finances correctly?
- What are the important dates I need to know when self-employed, e.g. tax return due dates, payment dates etc.?

THE NEXT STEP

THE NEXT STEP

5) FINANCIAL MANAGEMENT

STEP 5 – Financial Management

Post-graduation Expenditure

One of the hardest things to come to terms with, post-graduation, was the amount of money required BEFORE laying my hands on a patient or starting in a practice.

Here is an overview of the costs you may want to consider:
- GCC registration: £750 + (if you start work before 10 November of the graduating year)
  - £800 due again at the end of November of graduation year for the forthcoming year (so double whammy)
  - PLUS cost of passport photos, GP letter/report, stamps, envelopes etc.
- Association membership
- Insurance
  - Pro rata until December then full fee (approximately £400 until December, then around £800/£900 for the year, depending on the insurance company and if it's connected with an Association membership or not).
- Deposit for accommodation (usually 6 weeks rent)
  - PLUS one month's rent upfront
- If renting through an estate agent, there is usually a fee for application and an advanced payment on their 'exit check'. Also check if there are any other fees that may apply?
- Monthly rent/mortgage
- Contents insurance

THE NEXT STEP

- Monthly council tax (check band of property via local council website). You can get a 25% discount if you live alone. Again, check your local council website for further information.
- Bills – electric, gas, water, waste water, TV licence, internet, mobile phone
- Car – insurance, road tax, breakdown cover, petrol, tyres, service, MOT
- Food, mail redirection, entertainment, gym membership, clothes, lightbulbs and so forth
- Events – Christmas, holidays
- Dentist, doctor, and any other practitioners you may attend

Below, In Table 1, is an example of an expenditure excel spreadsheet showing an overview from the month of graduation and the following year. Each expense will of course be personal to you depending on the Association you choose, the insurance company that is attached to that Association, the CPD events you attend, your personal outgoings with accommodation, and so on.

Generally, the table illustrates that before you get started as a Chiropractor you should consider allowing approximately £5,000 to get you settled in a new area before you start working in your new profession. This isn't meant to panic you, but allow you to establish upfront finances for when you need them. It is therefore important to complete Exercise 15 to give you an overview of your own personal expected outgoings.

THE NEXT STEP

The biggest expense is therefore not registration, but moving to new accommodation. This can be overcome by sharing with someone or residing temporarily with family/friends until the necessary money is raised.

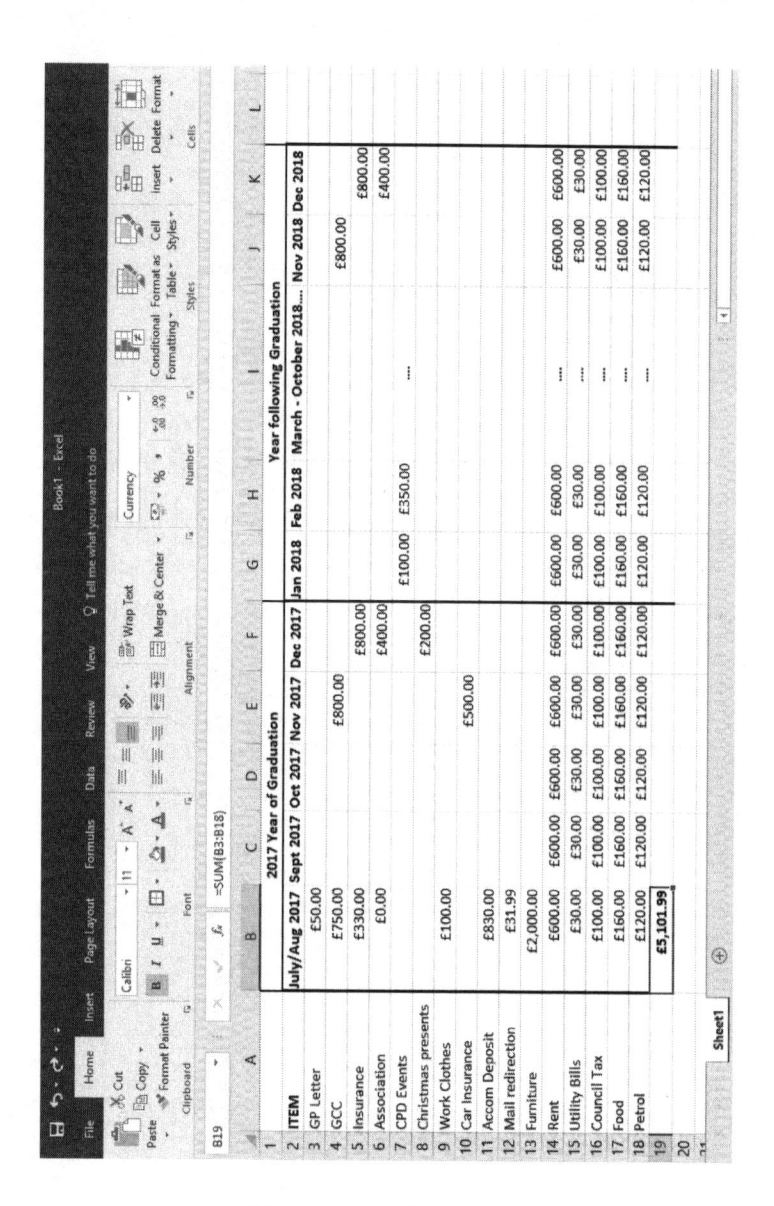

ITEM	2017 Year of Graduation					Year following Graduation				
	July/Aug 2017	Sept 2017	Oct 2017	Nov 2017	Dec 2017	Jan 2018	Feb 2018	March - October 2018....	Nov 2018	Dec 2018
GP Letter	£50.00									
GCC	£750.00									
Insurance	£330.00			£800.00					£800.00	
Association	£0.00				£400.00					£400.00
CPD Events					£200.00	£100.00	£350.00			
Christmas presents		£100.00								
Work Clothes				£500.00						
Car Insurance	£830.00									
Accom Deposit	£31.99									
Mall redirection										
Furniture	£2,000.00									
Rent	£600.00	£600.00	£600.00	£600.00	£600.00	£600.00	£600.00	...	£600.00	£600.00
Utility Bills	£30.00	£30.00	£30.00	£30.00	£30.00	£30.00	£30.00	...	£30.00	£30.00
Council Tax	£100.00	£100.00	£100.00	£100.00	£100.00	£100.00	£100.00	...	£100.00	£100.00
Food	£160.00	£160.00	£160.00	£160.00	£160.00	£160.00	£160.00	...	£160.00	£160.00
Petrol	£120.00	£120.00	£120.00	£120.00	£120.00	£120.00	£120.00	...	£120.00	£120.00
	£5,101.99									

Table 1: Expenditure Sheet.

THE NEXT STEP

Row 4:
The frequency of GCC payments if you register prior to 10 November of graduation year.

Rows 5–6:
The frequency of Association and insurance fees. These fee values are example figures and will vary depending on the Association and insurance you take out.

Row 8:
Don't forget to budget for Christmas with all the other outgoings. (That is if you celebrate Christmas and require a budget.)

Rows 9–10:
Other annual expenses that may apply to you.

Rows 11–13:
One off payment required to move into unfurnished accommodation.

Rows 14–18:
The accommodation outgoings you may encounter, depending on your personal circumstance, which will repeat monthly. Everyone's expenditure is different depending on their circumstances, whether they move home, live independently or house share, and the area they move to.

Row 19:
The total required to set up in a new area before even starting work in a practice and earning an income.

Exercise 15: Financial Overview

To gain an insight into your current financial status, answer the questions below.

QUESTIONS:
- What are my current outgoings on a weekly/monthly/annual basis?
  e.g. car, car insurance, food, registrations, beautician, hair, club fees/memberships, rent, phone, utility bills etc.
- What income do I have, if any?
- What savings do I have, if any?
- What helpful sources do I have? (e.g. family, post graduate loan and so forth)
- What needs to be put in place over the next few months?

Exercise 16: Expenditure Sheet Overview

Following on from Exercise 15, Create your own excel spreadsheet, as in Table 1 to calculate all eventualities.

Now that you have completed Exercises 15 and 16, you can gain financial control. Remember, at the end of the academic year your student loan has run out, and you're effectively 'broke' (unless you have been clever) and this is where you need to source finances from somewhere; whether savings, graduate bank loan, parental loan etc. You need to calculate and figure it out, either on your own or with someone supportive. Remember you may not get paid until the end of the first month worked, though this is dependent on the frequency you agree with the practice you work in.

Business Financial Management

Usually alongside a personal bank account (which you may have opened to use as your business account), is a high-interest savings account. I would encourage you to open this also. In this account, save your percentage tax each month to pay HMRC at the end of the year. You must not touch this, so you may as well earn some interest on it.

In this account, the day after 'pay day' place your:
- Income Tax (20%)
- Student Loan (9% if earn >£21,000)
- National Insurance (approximately 1%)
- Total = 30% (DO NOT TOUCH!!!)

At the time of earning, it seems you're taking a lot of money out of your income. But on tax day, you'll be grateful you've enough aside to pay the bill landing on your doormat. In fact, with a good accountant, after all expenses have been deducted, you're likely to have a nice bonus to reward yourself for the hard-earned hours of labour. You may find you're also able to pay your GCC fees, Association fees and insurance from this account each year.

Although I indicate above to save 30% off your whole _income_, the tax won't apply to your business expenses. But what counts as expenses is at the discretion of HMRC, therefore it's better to have too much in this account than too little. Remember this is not what

THE NEXT STEP

you <u>have</u> to do, but a recommendation, and it's worked well for me and others who have adopted this approach.

If you have a student bank account, it's also a good idea to change it to a 'graduate account', which can give you 0% overdraft up to £2,000 for 3 years depending on the terms and conditions of the bank.

Personal Financial Management

If you become self-employed, you are known as a sole trader. This means you're running your own business as an individual. You can keep all your 'business' profits after you've paid tax on them. So by removing the 30% from your account, the remainder is yours! What you choose to do with this money is up to you, however it's a good idea to compartmentalise things, so I recommend the following.

The remaining 70% in the business account now becomes 100%. Of the balance in that account, divide that 100% as follows:
- 50% is transferred in to your everyday personal account (as wages if you like) for rent, groceries, hairdressers, clothes, nights out etc.)
- 50% remains in the 'business account' for seminars, equipment, stationery, and all other business expenses.

THE NEXT STEP

The important message here is, put 30% away for tax purposes and **keep your 'business account' separate to your own personal spending!** Take time to figure out what works for you and adapt as necessary to your personal circumstances.

Student Loan

This information is based on UK residents with a UK-based student loan from the Student Loan Company (SLC) and is elaborated further on Martin Lewis' website: www.moneysavingexpert.com

The topic of student loan, leads on nicely from the previous discussion about finances. A lot of people are deterred from borrowing more money for fear of the ever-accumulative student loan. As Martin Lewis puts it, 'Think of it [student loan] like a graduate tax, not a loan'.

If you started your course after 2012, You repay 9% of everything earned **over** £21,000 a year. Therefore if you earn £30,000 a year gross (pre-tax) salary, you will repay £810 a year (£30,000 - £21,000 = £9,000 x 9% = £810) and that if you earn less than £21,000 you may not have to pay anything off the loan, unless you personally choose to. Be aware, however, of the interest rates that apply to your student loan. Further up-to-date information regarding your student loan can be found on www.slc.co.uk as well as the terms and conditions of your loan.

Graduates who started their course before September 2012, repay 9% of everything earned above £16,365. Those who started after 2012 and beyond, see it increased to £21,000.

THE NEXT STEP

The debt for those who started their course in September 2012 has a lifespan of 30 years, then the debt is wiped if you become permanently unfit to work or die [30 years from 01 April of the year after graduation when you were first due to repay]. For those who started before 2012, the loan has a twenty-five-year lifespan from 01 April of the year of graduation when you were first due to repay. For further information on student loans and how the repayment works, visit the student loans tuition fees section in www.moneysavingexpert.com

So don't panic about having to pay your student loan back immediately if you're from the UK. This will be looked after once you've completed your tax assessment, and if you have earned over the minimum amount. Make sure you inform HMRC and your accountant that you have a student loan prior to submission of the tax return. Also ensure you understand all the terms and conditions of a student loan, its repayment, and stay up-to-date with this information as the rules and amounts can change! Check the above websites for necessary information.

THE NEXT STEP

Exercise 17: Student Loan Management

Below is a list of questions you should know the answers to.

QUESTIONS:
- What are the terms and conditions of my SLC?
- Where are my log-in details for the SLC? – these are required long after graduation
- What are the contact details for my SLC?
- What up-to-date information is available on www.moneysavingexpert.com/students?

THE NEXT STEP

6 ANNUAL RESPONSIBILITIES

STEP 6 – Annual Responsibilities
Continuing Professional Development (CPD)

To retain registration with the GCC, you must undertake thirty hours of learning activity each year, spending fifteen of that total learning with colleagues and other professionals. The easiest way to participate in the 'learning with others' is to do seminars, though these can prove costly (again a business expense). You can also hold technique days with other Chiropractors, discussing cases etc., as long as this is documented and contains all the necessary information, and you have that documentation as proof of occurrence. Some Chiropractic seminars usually give a 'first year graduate' discount.

Once registered with the GCC, you get login details for their site. Under the CPD section there is a CPD booklet of requirements and an online form you must fill in when required to by GCC.

Each CPD year is 01 September to 31 August. If you graduate in July, you're exempt from submitting CPD to the GCC of *that* graduating year, so don't think you have to squash 30 hours CPD into one/two month(s). All CPD requirements for the following years must be submitted by 30 September; i.e. if you graduate in July 2017, your first submission of CPD will be due September 2018.

THE NEXT STEP

To submit CPD to the GCC, the 'learning cycle' must be completed outlining 'reflection, planning, undertaking and evaluation'.

Upon submission of the learning cycle, the GCC may audit your CPD. If this occurs, you are required to forward evidence of your CPD hours.

Remember to check the GCC website for up-to-date information on CPD.

Exercise 18: CPD Preparation

Answer the questions below to check where you have gaps in your knowledge about CPD.

QUESTIONS:
- How does CPD work and what is required from the GCC?
- When will I download, and read the CPD guidelines from the GCC website?
- What CPD will I participate in this year? What hours does this accumulate to?
- When does the CPD have to be submitted?
- Do I have evidence – should an audit be performed? Is this located in one place?

THE NEXT STEP

TIPS:
1. Read the CPD booklet once graduated and explore the website and requirement for learning cycle etc. in the beginning, so you can update your CPD folder consecutively, instead of trying to backtrack. Have a folder with an index at the beginning with titles: Date, [name of seminar], Location, CPD hours, Certificate/necessary proof enclosed. At the end of each CPD year, have a printout of the completed learning cycle sent to the GCC, so if an audit is requested, you have everything necessary without stress to photocopy and submit. All information is available on www.gcc-uk.org.
2. After each seminar, request a copy of the certificate immediately from those providing the seminar to place in the folder. Some Associations/courses don't automatically give you the certificate, or you have to download from their website which can be challenging when you've forgotten the password and need to contact them directly to reset, so get everything as you go along while it's fresh in your mind.
3. Keep your username and password for the GCC website (and any other websites e.g. SOTO Europe) in a secure accessible place. Realistically you may not remember these as you may only go onto the site a few times per year and the last thing you want is to miss deadlines due to not having your login.

HMRC

Book-keeping

So how do you record all this expenditure? There are many systems you can subscribe to, or indeed your accountant may have a personal system they prefer you use. However, my accountant, in the beginning, was quite happy with the excel sheet I created, which gave an understandable, clear overview. One thing I will say is... update this at the end of every week/month! There is nothing more tedious than filling out an excel sheet, cross-referencing with your bank account AND the receipts you've collected. It's tedious, however a necessity! If you do it weekly, it can take less than an hour. Leave it longer, and prepare for a long day indoors and it'll probably be sunny!

Once the relevant information is entered on the computer, store your business receipts in an envelope, and at the end of the month have them in chronological order on a metal ended treasury tag and compartmentalised into months. This sounds very OCD, however if you need to return something or want to check certain details, you can do a quick 'CTRL+ F' on the excel sheet, check the date and within seconds find the receipt required! It's easy if you do it from the start. However, you may have a better way, so do what works for you.

THE NEXT STEP

It's also a good idea to categorise your expenditure. For example:
- 'Training' for any CPD activities.
- 'Registrations' for Associations, GCC, RCoC etc.
- 'Insurance' for your Chiropractic Insurance and any other insurances you may have.

Exercise 19: Book Keeping

Answer the questions below to explore how you will manage your book keeping.

QUESTIONS:
- What system am I going to use to document income and expenditure?
- How often am I going to update this system?
- How will I organise the receipts as proof of expenditure?
- What 'categories' do I require to compartmentalise the expenditure?

Tax Return

If you're registered as self-employed, you must complete a tax return for HMRC. This can be done online or by post. If sent by post the deadline is 31 October. If sent online the deadline is 31 January. You'll receive a letter in April (tax year being April to April) to remind you of your tax return which needs to be completed and submitted either by you or your accountant by the above dates.

THE NEXT STEP

According to the HMRC website 'you'll get a penalty of £100 if your tax return is up to 3 months late. You'll have to pay more if it's later', so make sure you know those dates and make sure the accountant is on top of their responsibilities also. For further information on tax return deadlines and penalties visit: www.hmrc.gov.uk.

If you're going to submit your tax return yourself, or want to become familiar with the procedure, there's plenty of helpful information on the HMRC website, including videos. www.gov.uk/topic/personal-tax/self-assessment.

TIP:

Have an annual calendar of the necessary deadlines for tax return submission, tax payment, GCC payment, CPD deadline, Association payment, insurance payment, courses dates (with cost) and any other due dates for expenses.

THE NEXT STEP

Exercise 20: Tax Return

Below is information you may want to obtain in preparation for tax submission.

QUESTIONS:
- What dates do I need to be aware of for my tax return?
- What documents/requirements do I need in place to submit a tax return?
- Who do I need to talk to, to either complete a tax return or authorise its submission?

National Insurance

According to the HMRC website, 'National Insurance contributions are paid to build up your entitlement to certain state benefits, i.e. your State Pension. The contributions you pay depend on how much you earn and whether you're employed or self-employed. Once you reach pension age, you stop paying National Insurance'. At present (2016) there are two types of National Insurance to pay when self-employed. Class 2 and Class 4. Class 2 National Insurance is £2.80/week if you earn more than £5,965 per annum. Class 4 is calculated at 9% on profits between £8,060 and £43,000 and 2% on profits greater than £43,000 Further information can be found at www.hmrc.gov.uk.

THE NEXT STEP

Income tax

Income Tax is the tax you pay on your income. Nearly everyone residing in the UK receives a Personal Allowance of £11,000 (for 2016–2017) and £11,200 (in 2017–2018) tax free according to the HMRC website, therefore Income Tax is only due on taxable income that's above your tax-free allowance. Below is a summary for 2016–2017 of the tax percentage required to be paid on earning certain income:

- First £11,000 = tax free
- £11,000–£43,000 = 20% on income, 20% on savings and 10% on dividends
- £43,000–150K = 40% on income, 40% on savings and 32.5% on dividends
- >£150k = 45% on income, 45% on savings and 37.5% on dividends

For further up-to-date detailed information on the above, visit www.hmrc.gov.uk

VAT

Chiropractic is currently VAT exempt due to it being a Healthcare Profession. If you are selling equipment or products, however, you may need to ask your accountant or HMRC whether you need to become 'part-exempt'.

THE NEXT STEP

THE NEXT STEP

7. BEING TRUE TO YOU!

THE NEXT STEP

STEP 7 – Being True to You!

A lot of students become associates because it's the best marked path upon graduation. Sometimes associates find they aren't making enough money, not getting enough support, and find themselves stuck in this position. It's either due to fear of moving, the contract they are tied to, or they feel they cannot afford to leave and don't want to give up 'too soon', but the truth is – *what doesn't work for you works against you.*

I was informed that the first two years, post-graduation, were like the apprenticeship years, and there are two objectives to those years: to learn, and to make money. When you stop learning on the job you're in, especially if you are not happy, you should move on! If you're in a good practice, the learning will not stop, you'll be supported and you'll grow into a well-rounded Chiropractor.

If you find you're not looking forward to going to work, or have any inkling of dread associated with the job, you can't learn like that and you go into fight/flight protective mode instead of growth mode. You become self-preserving instead of flourishing. Remember the mantra 'business is business', and don't let anyone emotionally guilt trip you into staying if you're not happy.

I've been in that 'stuck' place (more in my mind than real). The 'what if' questions were popping through my head: 'what if I get a bad reputation; or can't find another job; or I'm being dumb and going to fail?' I stayed in that position, not going forward, and in the end felt I was moving backwards to the point where I started to doubt not only myself but my profession.

THE NEXT STEP

The above example demonstrates the importance of congruency. It's important to find somewhere you can be faithful to your mission, your values and your vision. If you step into someone else's vision, and it is pressed upon you, and you don't agree with it, the relationship will deteriorate, often rapidly. If you find yourself here, do both parties a favour and get out. You (and they) will be thankful you did. 'Do what is hard to make life easy!' and never live your life by someone else's standards or goals unless they coincide.

Remember 'FEAR' stands for 'False Expectations Appearing Real'. As the American psychologist Susan Jeffers says 'feel the fear and do it anyway'. When you look back, hindsight being the great thing that it is, you'll be glad you let go of what was holding you back.

Build yourself up. You're building upon a very strong foundation – the one that got you into Chiropractic College and the skills you learned there. Granted, over the period of your education, your vision may have become diluted, but having done the exercise throughout the book, your vision and direction should be clear.

You came out of the womb knowing nothing except survival. *Everything* has been a learned skill. You have the ability, all you need to do is start, organise, practise and ask yourself the right questions. If you continue practising what doesn't fit your vision, mission and values, you will negligibly reinforce your journey. As the saying goes 'If you don't get off the road you're on, you may end up where you're headed'.

THE NEXT STEP

If you're stuck, find someone who knows what they're doing in the area you need help and ask, observe and learn, YouTube, Google, watch videos – whatever! Get a clear vision of your direction and move forward.

Follow a proven system and adapt it to suit you. Who do you know in the industry who has a practice which you admire? Find someone, a mentor who can lead you into the business world without you trying to re-invent the wheel.

Most importantly, enjoy being a Chiropractor. You have the skills, you have the training, you have the intelligence to adapt, change, improve and learn. Take action and MAKE THE CHANGE.

There's a reason you decided to become a Chiropractor. Keep that alight and have fun. Be YOU, be strong, and help those who need YOU!

THE NEXT STEP

Index of Websites (in alphabetical order)

Anglo European College of Chiropractic (AECC)
www.aecc.ac.uk/

British Chiropractic Association (BCA)
https://chiropractic-uk.co.uk/

General Chiropractic Council (GCC)
https://www.gcc-uk.org/

HMRC
https://www.gov.uk/government/organisations/hm-revenue-customs

McTimoney College of Chiropractic
www.mctimoney-college.ac.uk/

MoneySavingExpert.com
www.moneysavingexpert.com

Scottish Chiropractic Association (SCA)
www.sca-chiropractic.org/

The Royal College of Chiropractors (RCC)
www.rcc-uk.org/

United Chiropractic Association (UCA)
www.united-chiropractic.org/

Welsh Institute of Chiropractic (WIOC)
http://wioc.southwales.ac.uk/